IN GOD
WE
TRUST

QUOTATIONS, THOUGHTS,
AND PRAYERS FOR
THE 2008 ELECTIONS

IN GOD WE TRUST

QUOTATIONS, THOUGHTS,
AND PRAYERS FOR
THE 2008 ELECTIONS

BARBOUR
PUBLISHING

© 2008 by Barbour Publishing, Inc.

ISBN 978-1-60260-022-5

Published by Barbour Publishing, Inc., P.O. Box 719, Uhrichsville, Ohio 44683, www.barbourbooks.com

Our mission is to publish and distribute inspirational products offering exceptional value and biblical encouragement to the masses.

Printed in the United States of America.

CONTENTS

Introduction: In God We Trust 7
V: Victory over Oppression 9
O: One Nation under God. 23
T: The Right to Choose 47
E: Extending the Experiment 61
Final Thoughts: Do Your Duty! 89

Introduction:
In God We Trust

Politics can be tricky.

Sure, there are a lot of greedy, underhanded people in our government. Some officials are incompetent, others downright wicked. But there are also many honest and capable folks who truly want to serve their fellow citizens. In spite of pressures and trials, they seek office, work hard, and do everything in their power to better our nation.

In a cynical age, it's easy to focus on the one group while overlooking the other. But that's not the Christian way. Throughout the Bible, we are told to respect our rulers, to be submissive to them, and to pray for them. Why? Because, ultimately, "there is no authority except that which God has established" (Romans 13:1).

In the United States, Christians enjoy the unusual opportunity of working *with* God in the selection of our leaders. Because our government was founded on the idea of the "consent of the governed," we have the right to vote for those individuals we believe will best serve our nation—under the guidance of the powerful God who "sets up kings and deposes them" (Daniel 2:21).

With another important election approaching, this book will challenge and encourage you to do your duty—as an American citizen and as a follower of Jesus Christ. Organized according to the acronym VOTE, you'll read eloquent thoughts on

Victory over Oppression—our *founding*
One Nation under God—our *Friend*
The Right to Choose—our *freedoms*
Extending the Experiment—our *future*

Each section will remind you of your privilege and entitlement to be part of the electoral process. Each section also calls to mind the overarching principle of God's leadership in national affairs. Though we may not like the result of every election or agree with each action of our leaders, we can know that God Himself—in His own way—is working out His plan for our nation.

Salvation never comes from Washington, Sacramento, Albany, or Columbus. Our lives don't depend on presidents, senators, or members of congress. Though each is important, our bedrock belief is simply this: *In God We Trust*.

VICTORY OVER OPPRESSION
OUR *FOUNDING*

What many of us take for granted today was a revolutionary idea in 1776: that human beings could and should govern themselves as a nation. Note the emphasis Thomas Jefferson, in the Declaration of Independence, put on freedom as a gift of "Nature's God":

When in the course of human events, it becomes necessary for one people to dissolve the political bands which have connected them with another, and to assume among the powers of the earth, the separate and equal station to which the laws of nature and of nature's God entitle them, a decent respect to the opinions of mankind requires that they should declare the causes which impel them to the separation.

We hold these truths to be self-evident, that all men are created equal, that they are endowed by their Creator with certain unalienable rights, that among these are life, liberty and the pursuit of happiness.

The Declaration of Independence, continued

That to secure these rights, governments are instituted among men, deriving their just powers from the consent of the governed.

That whenever any form of government becomes destructive of these ends, it is the right of the people to alter or to abolish it, and to institute new government, laying its foundations on such principles and organizing its powers in such form, as to them shall seem most likely to effect their safety and happiness. . . .

The Declaration of Independence, continued

We, therefore, the representatives of the united States of America, in general congress, assembled, appealing to the Supreme Judge of the world for the rectitude of our intentions, do, in the name, and by authority of the good people of these colonies, solemnly publish and declare, that these united colonies are, and of right ought to be free and independent states...

And for the support of this Declaration, with a firm reliance on the protection of Divine Providence, we mutually pledge to each other our lives, our fortunes, and our sacred honor.

We have this day restored the Sovereign
to whom all men ought to be obedient.
He reigns in heaven and from the rising
to the setting of the sun, let His Kingdom come.

SAMUEL ADAMS

The Declaration of Independence
first organized the social compact
on the foundation of the Redeemer's mission. . . .
[I]t laid the cornerstone of human government
upon the first precepts of Christianity.

JOHN QUINCY ADAMS

FROM A SPEECH COMMEMORATING

THE DECLARATION OF INDEPENDENCE,

JULY 4, 1837

*Men must choose
to be governed by God,
or condemn themselves
to be ruled by tyrants.*

WILLIAM PENN

*Freedom is not a gift bestowed upon us by other men,
but a right that belongs to us
by the laws of God and nature. . . .
I never doubted the existence of the Deity,
that He made the world,
and governed it by His Providence. . . .
The pleasures of this world are rather
from God's goodness than our own merit. . . .
Whoever shall introduce into the public affairs
the principles of primitive Christianity
will change the face of the world.*

BENJAMIN FRANKLIN

You have rights antecedent to all earthly governments; rights that cannot be repealed or restrained by human laws; rights derived from the Great Legislator of the universe.

JOHN ADAMS

The God who gave us life gave us liberty. And can the liberties of a nation be thought secure when we have removed their only firm basis, a conviction in the minds of the people that these liberties are of the gift of God?

Thomas Jefferson

*It cannot be emphasized too strongly or too often
that this great nation was founded
not by religionists but by Christians,
not on religion but on the gospel of Jesus Christ.
We shall not fight alone.
God presides over the destinies of nations.
The battle is not to the strong alone.
Is life so dear, or peace so sweet,
as to be purchased at the price of chains and slavery?
Forbid it, ALMIGHTY GOD!
Give me liberty or give me death!*

PATRICK HENRY

The highest glory of the American Revolution was this: it connected in one indissoluble bond the principles of civil government with the principles of Christianity. From the day of the Declaration. . .they [the American people] were bound by the laws of God, which they all, and by the laws of the gospel, which they nearly all, acknowledge as the rules of their conduct.

John Quincy Adams

Congress shall make no law respecting an establishment of religion, or prohibiting the free exercise thereof. . . .

AMENDMENT I

BILL OF RIGHTS

U.S. CONSTITUTION

ONE NATION UNDER GOD
OUR *FRIEND*

Many of us grew up reciting the Pledge of Allegiance in school and other settings—from 4-H clubs to church. In only thirty-one words, the Pledge reminds us of our nation, its benefits, and the God who oversees them all:

I pledge allegiance to the flag
of the United States of America,
and to the republic for which it stands,
one nation under God, indivisible,
with liberty and justice for all.

The words "under God" were added to the pledge by Congress in 1954.

In this way we are reaffirming
the transcendence of religious faith
in America's heritage and future;
in this way we shall constantly strengthen
those spiritual weapons which forever will be
our country's most powerful resource in peace and war.

DWIGHT D. EISENHOWER

FROM A 1954 SPEECH AFTER CONGRESS AMENDED
THE PLEDGE OF ALLEGIANCE TO ADD
THE WORDS "UNDER GOD"

Long before Congress acknowledged God in the Pledge of Allegiance, Benjamin Franklin sought the help of "that powerful Friend" during the Constitutional Convention of 1787:

In this situation of this assembly, groping, as it were, in the dark to find political truth, and scarce able to distinguish it when presented to us, how has it happened, sir, that we have not hitherto once thought of humbly applying to the Father of Lights to illuminate our understandings? In the beginning of the contest with Britain, when we were sensible of danger, we had daily prayers in this room for the Divine protection. Our prayers, sir, were heard; they were graciously answered. . . . Have we now forgotten that powerful Friend?

Benjamin Franklin, continued

...I have lived, sir, a long time; and the longer I live, the more convincing proofs I see of this truth, that God governs in the affairs of men. And if a sparrow cannot fall to the ground without His notice, is it probable that an empire can rise without His aid?

Benjamin Franklin, continued

We have been assured, sir, in the sacred writings, that "except the Lord build the house, they labor in vain that build it." I firmly believe this; and I also believe, that without His concurring aid, we shall succeed in this political building no better than the builders of Babel; we shall be divided by our little, partial, local interests, our projects will be confounded, and we ourselves shall become a reproach and a byword to future ages. And what is worse, mankind may hereafter, from this unfortunate instance, despair of establishing government by human wisdom, and leave it to chance, war, and conquest.

Benjamin Franklin, continued

I therefore beg leave to move that henceforth
prayers, imploring the assistance of heaven and
its blessing on our deliberations, be held in this
Assembly every morning before we proceed to
business; and that one or more of the clergy of
this city be requested to officiate in that service.

IN GOD WE TRUST

ONE NATION UNDER GOD'

*In his first inaugural address in 1789, President
George Washington also begged the blessings of God
upon the new nation:*

It would be peculiarly improper to omit, in this
first official act, my fervent supplication to that
Almighty Being, who rules over the universe,
who presides in the councils of nations, and
whose providential aids can supply every human defect, that His benediction may consecrate
to the liberties and happiness of the people of
the United States, a government instituted by
themselves for these essential purposes: and may
enable every instrument employed in its admin-
istration to execute success, the functions allotted
to his charge. In tendering this homage to the
Great Author of every public and private good,
I assure myself that it expresses your sentiments
not less than my own.

George Washington, continued

No people can be bound to acknowledge and adore the invisible hand which conducts the affairs of men more than the people of the United States. Every step by which they have advanced to the character of an independent nation seems to have been distinguished by some token of providential agency.... We ought to be no less persuaded that the propitious smiles of heaven can never be expected on a nation that disregards the eternal rules of order and right, which heaven itself has ordained.

During the United States' first presidential inaugural, George Washington added a phrase to the Constitutional oath of office, which reads as follows:

I do solemnly swear (or affirm) that I will faithfully execute the office of President of the United States, and will to the best of my ability, preserve, protect, and defend the Constitution of the United States.

U.S. CONSTITUTION

ARTICLE II, SECTION 1

Washington added, "So help me God," an example followed by most other presidents.

George Washington issued a proclamation of thanksgiving in October 1789 that emphasized, once again, his belief that the United States should clearly acknowledge God's role in its national well-being.

Whereas it is the duty of all nations to acknowledge the providence of Almighty God, to obey His will, to be grateful for His benefits, and humbly to implore His protection and favor, and whereas both houses of Congress have by their joint committee requested me "to recommend to the people of the United States a day of public thanksgiving and prayer to be observed by acknowledging with grateful hearts that many signal favors of Almighty God, especially by affording them an opportunity peaceably to establish a form of government for their safety and happiness."

Washington's proclamation of thanksgiving, continued

Now therefore I do recommend and assign Thursday the twenty-sixth day of November next to be devoted by the people of these States to the service of that great and glorious Being, who is the beneficent Author of all the good that was, that is, or that will be. That we may then all unite in rendering unto Him our sincere and humble thanks, for His kind care and protection of the people of this country previous to their becoming a nation, for the signal and manifold mercies, and the favorable interpositions of His providence, which we experienced in the course and conclusion of the late war, for the great degree of tranquility, union, and plenty, which we have since enjoyed, for the peaceable and rational manner in which we have been enabled to establish constitutions of government for our safety and happiness, and particularly the national one now lately instituted, for the civil and religious liberty with which we are blessed, and the means we have of acquiring and diffusing useful knowledge and in general for all the great and various favors which He hath been pleased to confer upon us.

Washington's proclamation of thanksgiving, continued

And also that we may then unite in most humbly offering our prayers and supplications to the great Lord and Ruler of nations and beseech Him to pardon our national and other transgressions, to enable us all, whether in public or private stations, to perform our several and relative duties properly and punctually, to render our national government a blessing to all the people, by constantly being a government of wise, just and constitutional laws, discreetly and faithfully executed and obeyed, to protect and guide all sovereigns and nations (especially such as have shown kindness to us) and to bless them with good government, peace, and concord. To promote the knowledge and practice of true religion and virtue. . . .

These are the things that remain constant.
These are the things that unite us.
There are other eternal truths,
other eternal constants in our lives:
our constant devotion to the principles of
freedom, democracy and the free enterprise system;
our constant belief in the promise of this
country that the best is yet to come;
a country that exists by
the grace of Divine Providence—
Divine Providence that gave us this land
and told us to be good stewards of it
and good stewards of each other.
The land that God has truly,
truly blessed and that we are
proud to call AMERICA!

COLIN POWELL

1996 REPUBLICAN CONVENTION

*Belief in,
and dependence on,
God is absolutely
essential.*

RONALD REAGAN

It is the duty of nations,
as well as of men,
to own their dependence
upon the overruling power of God. . .
and to recognize the sublime truth
announced in the Holy Scriptures
and proven by all history,
that those nations only are blessed
whose God is the Lord.

ABRAHAM LINCOLN

The Almighty God has blessed our land in many ways.
He has given our people stout hearts
and strong arms with which to strike
mighty blows for freedom and truth.
He has given to our country a faith
which has become the hope of all peoples
in an anguished world.

FRANKLIN D. ROOSEVELT

FOURTH PRESIDENTIAL INAUGURAL ADDRESS

JANUARY 20, 1945

*We ask almighty God
to watch over our nation. . .
and may He always guide
our country.*

GEORGE W. BUSH

SEPTEMBER 14, 2001

*There are a good many problems
before the American people today,
and before me as president,
but I expect to find the solution
of those problems just in the proportion
that I am faithful in the study of the
Word of God.*

WOODROW WILSON

Scripture says:
"Blessed are those who mourn for
they shall be comforted."
I call on every American family
and the family of America
to observe a National Day of Prayer
and Remembrance...
We will persevere...
In time, we will find healing and recovery;
and, in the face of all this evil,
we remain strong and united,
"one Nation under God."

GEORGE W. BUSH

AFTER THE TERRORIST ATTACKS OF
SEPTEMBER 11, 2001

"The Star Spangled Banner" is familiar to most Americans, if for no other reason than that it's sung before most sporting events. But author Francis Scott Key wrote an additional verse that honors God as the true friend of the United States:

O! thus be it ever when freemen shall stand,

Between their lov'd home, and the war's desolation,

Blest with vict'ry and peace, may the Heav'n
    rescued land,

Praise the Power that hath made and preserv'd
    us a nation!

Then conquer we must, when our cause it is just,

And this be our motto—"In God is our Trust";

And the star-spangled banner in triumph shall wave

O'er the land of the free and the home of the brave!

Our fathers' God to Thee,
author of liberty,
to Thee we sing.

SAMUEL F. SMITH
"AMERICA"

THE RIGHT TO CHOOSE
OUR *FREEDOMS*

As we approach another presidential election, it's worth considering the words of the traditional march with which we greet our President:

Yours is the aim to make this grand country
    grander,
This you will do, that's our strong, firm belief.
Hail to the one we selected as commander,
Hail to the President! Hail to the Chief!

*Providence has given our people
the choice of their rulers,
and it is the duty as well as the privilege and interest
of our Christian nation to select and
prefer Christians for their rulers.*

JOHN JAY

FIRST CHIEF JUSTICE OF THE
U.S. SUPREME COURT

*The choice before us is plain, Christ or chaos,
conviction or compromise, discipline or disintegration.
I am rather tired of hearing about our rights
and privileges as American citizens.
The time is come, it now is,
when we ought to hear about the duties
and responsibilities of our citizenship.
America's future depends upon her accepting and
demonstrating God's government.*

PETER MARSHALL

SENATE CHAPLAIN FROM 1947 UNTIL
HIS DEATH IN 1949

The freedom to choose our leaders is written into the earliest pages of our nation's founding documents. Consider Article 1, Section 2 of the United States Constitution:

The House of Representatives shall be composed of members chosen every second year by the people of the several states. . . .

Through these elected officials, the people of the United States are represented in the affairs of the nation.

Additional voting guarantees have been written into the Constitution, by way of amendments. Here is the 15th Amendment, assuring that former slaves could cast ballots:

The right of citizens of the United States to vote shall not be denied or abridged by the United States or by any state on account of race, color, or previous condition of servitude.

*Passed by Congress February 26, 1869
Ratified by the states February 3, 1870*

The 17th Amendment to the U.S. Constitution brought the selection of senators directly to "we the people," rather than indirectly through our state legislatures.

The Senate of the United States shall be composed of two senators from each state, elected by the people thereof, for six years. . . .

Passed by Congress May 13, 1912
Ratified by the states April 8, 1913

The 19th Amendment guaranteed that women would have equal access to the voting booth.

The right of citizens of the United States to vote shall not be denied or abridged by the United States or by any state on account of sex.

Passed by Congress June 4, 1919
Ratified by the states August 18, 1920

The 26th Amendment allowed more people to vote by lowering the voting age.

The right of citizens of the United States, who are eighteen years of age or older, to vote shall not be denied or abridged by the United States or by any state on account of age.

Passed by Congress March 23, 1971
Ratified by the states July 1, 1971

To make democracy work,
we must be a nation of participants,
not simply observers.
One who does not vote
has no right to complain.

LOUIS L'AMOUR

Actually, with the Constitutional guarantee of freedom of speech, you would *have a right to complain. But your complaints will be more credible if you've made the effort to vote!*

From the Declaration of Independence:

We hold these truths to be self-evident, that all men are created equal, that they are endowed by their Creator with certain unalienable rights, that among these are life, liberty and the pursuit of happiness. That to secure these rights, governments are instituted among men, deriving their just powers from the consent of the governed...

From the Declaration of Independence, continued.

We, therefore, the representatives of the united States of America, in general congress, assembled, appealing to the Supreme Judge of the world for the rectitude of our intentions, do, in the name, and by authority of the good people of these colonies, solemnly publish and declare, that these united colonies are, and of right ought to be free and independent states.

EXTENDING THE EXPERIMENT
OUR FUTURE

Should people of faith care about politics, government, and elections? Consider these words of one of the founding fathers, James Madison.

We have staked the future of all our political institutions upon the capacity of mankind for self-government; upon the capacity of each and all of us to govern ourselves, to control ourselves, to sustain ourselves according to the Ten Commandments of God.

Through the generations, Christian faith has been extolled as a pillar of good citizenship.

While the law allows the American people to do everything, there are things which religion prevents them from imagining and forbids them to dare.

Religion, which never intervenes directly in the government of American society, should therefore be considered as the first of their political institutions, for although it did not give them a taste for liberty, it singularly facilitates their use thereof. . . .

For the Americans the ideas of Christianity and liberty are so completely mingled that it is almost impossible to get them to conceive of the one without the other.

Alexis de Tocqueville
Democracy in America, 1835

*The religion which has introduced civil liberty
is the religion of Christ and His apostles. . . .
This is genuine Christianity
and to this we owe our
free constitutions of government.*

NOAH WEBSTER

Every thinking man, when he thinks,
realizes that the teachings of the Bible
are so interwoven and entwined with our whole
civic and social life that it would be literally—
I do not mean figuratively, but literally—
impossible for us to figure what that loss would
be if these teachings were removed.
We would lose all the standards by which
we now judge both public and private morals;
all the standards towards which we, with more or
less resolution, strive to raise ourselves.

Theodore Roosevelt

*The fundamental basis of this nation's law
was given to Moses on the Mount.
The fundamental basis of our Bill of Rights
comes from the teaching we get from Exodus
and St. Matthew, from Isaiah and St. Paul.
I don't think we emphasize that enough these days.*

Harry S. Truman

*The moral principles and precepts
contained in the scriptures
ought to form the basis of all our civil
constitutions and laws.
All the miseries and evils which men suffer
from vice, crime, ambition, injustice,
oppression, slavery and war,
proceed from their despising or neglecting
the precepts contained in the Bible.*

NOAH WEBSTER

*In no other place in the United States
are there so many, and such varied
official evidences of deep and abiding faith
in God on the part of Governments as there
are in Washington. . . . Inasmuch as our great
leaders have shown no doubt about God's
proper place in the American birthright,
can we, in our day, dare do less?*

SENATOR ROBERT BYRD, 1962

The insightful nineteenth-century French writer Alexis de Tocqueville understood the underlying strength of the United States:

I sought for the greatness and the genius of America in her commodious harbors and her ample rivers—it was not there; in her fertile fields and boundless prairies, and it was not there; in her rich mines and her vast world commerce, and it was not there. Not until I went into the churches of America and heard her pulpits ablaze with righteousness did I meet the secret of her genius and power. America is great because she is good, and if America ever ceases to be good, America will cease to be great.

*The only limit to our realization
of tomorrow
will be our doubts of today.
Let us move forward
with strong and
active faith.*

FRANKLIN D. ROOSEVELT

Often times, our forward progress depends on a backwards look—especially to our true "founding document," the Bible. John Quincy Adams said:

So great is my veneration of the Bible,
that the earlier my children begin to read it
the more confident will be my hope that they
will prove useful citizens of their country
and respectable members of society.

*The more profoundly we study
this wonderful Book,
and the more closely
we observe its divine precepts,
the better citizens we will become
and the higher will be
our destiny as a nation.*

William McKinley

*The Bible is the Rock
on which this Republic rests.*

ANDREW JACKSON

*The Bible is endorsed by the ages.
Our civilization is built upon its words.
In no other Book is there such a collection
of inspired wisdom, reality and hope.*

DWIGHT D. EISENHOWER

Within the covers of the Bible
are all the answers
for all the problems men face.
The Bible can touch hearts,
order minds and refresh souls.

RONALD REAGAN

"Sanctify them by the truth; your word is truth."

JOHN 17:17

*"Then you will know the truth,
and the truth will set you free."*

JOHN 8:32

*Whatever makes men good Christians,
makes them good citizens.*

DANIEL WEBSTER

*Liberty cannot be established without morality,
nor morality without faith.*

HORACE GREELEY

*God grants liberty only to those who love it,
and are always ready to guard and defend it.*

DANIEL WEBSTER

If we fail now,
we shall have forgotten in abundance
what we learned in hardship:
that democracy rests on faith,
that freedom asks more than it gives,
and that the judgment of God is harshest
on those who are most favored.

Lyndon Baines Johnson

Inaugural Address, 1965

In 1863, during the depths of the Civil War, Abraham Lincoln called upon Americans to observe a national day of fasting, humiliation, and prayer. His words, spoken nearly 150 years ago, are amazingly relevant today:

We have been the recipients of the choicest bounties of heaven. We have been preserved, these many years, in peace and prosperity. We have grown in numbers, wealth, and power, as no other nation has ever grown. But we have forgotten God.

Abraham Lincoln, continued

We have forgotten the gracious hand which preserved us in peace, and multiplied and enriched and strengthened us; and we have vainly imagined, in the deceitfulness of our hearts, that all these blessings were produced by some superior wisdom and virtue of our own. Intoxicated with unbroken success, we have become too self-sufficient to feel the necessity of redeeming and preserving grace, too proud to pray to the God that made us.

It behooves us, then, to humble ourselves before the offended Power, to confess our national sins, and to pray for clemency and forgiveness.

*"If my people, who are called by my name,
will humble themselves and pray and seek
my face and turn from their wicked ways,
then will I hear from heaven
and will forgive their sin
and will heal their land."*

2 CHRONICLES 7:14

Tyranny is so generally established
in the rest of the world that
the prospect of an asylum in America
for those who love liberty gives general joy,
and our cause is esteemed the cause of all mankind. . . .
We are fighting for the dignity and
happiness of human nature.
Glorious it is for the Americans
to be called by Providence to this post of honor.

BENJAMIN FRANKLIN

Mine eyes have seen the glory of
the coming of the Lord;
He is trampling out the vintage
where the grapes of wrath are stored;
He hath loosed the fateful lightning
of His terrible swift sword:
His truth is marching on.

In the beauty of the lilies Christ
was born across the sea,
With a glory in His bosom that
transfigures you and me:
As he died to make men holy,
let us die to make men free,
While God is marching on.

JULIA WARD HOWE

"THE BATTLE HYMN OF THE REPUBLIC"

Whatever your political leaning, whoever your favorite candidate may be, the words of Abraham Lincoln provide a stirring example of trust in God for the nation's future. The sixteenth president said the following in his second inaugural address, toward the end of the Civil War:

Neither party expected for the war the magnitude or the duration which it has already attained. Neither anticipated that the *cause* of the conflict might cease with, or even before, the conflict itself should cease. Each looked for an easier triumph, and a result less fundamental and astounding. Both read the same Bible and pray to the same God, and each invokes His aid against the other. It may seem strange that any men should dare to ask a just God's assistance in wringing their bread from the sweat of other men's faces, but let us judge not, that we be not judged.

Lincoln's second inaugural address, continued

The prayers of both could not be answered. That of neither has been answered fully. The Almighty has His own purposes. "Woe unto the world because of offenses; for it must needs be that offenses come, but woe to that man by whom the offense cometh." If we shall suppose that American slavery is one of those offenses which, in the providence of God, must needs come, but which, having continued through His appointed time, He now wills to remove, and that He gives to both North and South this terrible war as the woe due to those by whom the offense came, shall we discern therein any departure from those divine attributes which the believers in a living God always ascribe to Him?

Lincoln's second inaugural address, continued

Fondly do we hope, fervently do we pray, that this mighty scourge of war may speedily pass away. Yet, if God wills that it continue until all the wealth piled by the bondsman's two hundred and fifty years of unrequited toil shall be sunk, and until every drop of blood drawn with the lash shall be paid by another drawn with the sword, as was said three thousand years ago, so still it must be said "the judgments of the Lord are true and righteous altogether."

*Blessed is the nation
whose God is the* LORD.

PSALM 33:12

FINAL THOUGHTS
DO YOUR DUTY!

Though the idea of a "popular vote" was centuries in the future in Jesus' time, the Lord Himself encouraged His followers to support both the earthly and heavenly governments.

"Give to Caesar what is Caesar's,
and to God what is God's."
MATTHEW 22:21

Christians in the United States have both the duty and the privilege of voting. Consider the apostle Paul's views on our relationship to our government:

Everyone must submit himself to the governing authorities, for there is no authority except that which God has established. The authorities that exist have been established by God. Consequently, he who rebels against the authority is rebelling against what God has instituted, and those who do so will bring judgment on themselves. For rulers hold no terror for those who do right, but for those who do wrong.

The apostle Paul, continued

Do you want to be free from fear of the one in authority? Then do what is right and he will commend you. For he is God's servant to do you good. But if you do wrong, be afraid, for he does not bear the sword for nothing. He is God's servant, an agent of wrath to bring punishment on the wrongdoer. Therefore, it is necessary to submit to the authorities, not only because of possible punishment but also because of conscience.

The apostle Paul, continued

This is also why you pay taxes, for the authorities are God's servants, who give their full time to governing. Give everyone what you owe him: If you owe taxes, pay taxes; if revenue, then revenue; if respect, then respect; if honor, then honor.

Romans 13:1–7

*"Seek the peace and prosperity of the city
to which I have carried you. . . .
Pray to the LORD for it,
because if it prospers,
you too will prosper."*

JEREMIAH 29:7

If you enjoy history,
look for
Fascinating Facts of the Faith
from Barbour Publishing!

Featuring 365 daily readings from Christian history, this book ranges from St. Augustine to Mount Zion; *Ben-Hur* to Beverly LaHaye; "A Mighty Fortress Is Our God" to *Veggie Tales*.

The Christian world boasts a wide variety of intriguing, inspiring, and influential people, places, and things. *Fascinating Facts of the Faith* provides brief, easy-to-read entries for every day of the year, giving readers insight into the growth and development of Christianity from the early church until now.

ISBN 978-1-60260-013-3
384 pages
5 ¼" x 8 ¼"
Paperback
$9.97

Available wherever Christian books are sold.